# We Need
# Teachers

by Jane Scoggins Bauld

Consulting Editor: Gail Saunders-Smith, Ph.D.

Consultant: Max Laird, President,
North Dakota Education Association

## Pebble Books

an imprint of Capstone Press
Mankato, Minnesota

Pebble Books are published by Capstone Press,
1710 Roe Crest Drive, North Mankato, Minnesota 56003.
www.capstonepub.com

Copyright © 2000 Capstone Press, a Capstone imprint. All rights reserved.
No part of this publication may be reproduced in whole or in part,
or stored in a retrieval system, or transmitted in any form or by any means,
electronic, mechanical, photocopying, recording, or otherwise,
without written permission of the publisher.
For information regarding permission, write to Capstone Press,
1710 Roe Crest Drive, North Mankato, Minnesota 56003.

*Library of Congress Cataloging-in-Publication Data*
Bauld, Jane Scoggins.
    We need teachers/by Jane Scoggins Bauld.
    p. cm.—(Helpers in our school)
    Includes bibliographical references and index.
    Summary: Simple text and photographs present teachers and their role in
elementary schools.
    ISBN-13: 978-0-7368-0533-9 (hardcover)
    ISBN-10: 0-7368-0533-8 (hardcover)
    ISBN-13: 978-0-7368-8717-5 (paperback)
    ISBN-10: 0-7368-8717-2 (paperback)
    1. Teachers—Juvenile literature. [1. Teachers. 2. Occupations.] I. Title. II. Series.
LB1775 .B364   2000
372.11—dc21                                                              99-046802

# Note to Parents and Teachers

The Helpers in Our School series supports national social studies
standards for how groups and institutions work to meet individual
needs. This book describes teachers and illustrates what they do in
schools. The photographs support early readers in understanding
the text. The repetition of words and phrases helps early readers
learn new words. This book also introduces early readers to subject-
specific vocabulary words, which are defined in the Words to Know
section. Early readers may need assistance to read some words and
to use the Table of Contents, Words to Know, Read More, Internet
Sites, and Index/Word List sections of the book.

Printed in the United States of America in North Mankato, Minnesota.
072012     006848R

# Table of Contents

Teachers help
students learn.

Teachers set up classrooms.

Teachers gather supplies.

Teachers plan lessons.

Teachers grade homework.

Scientists at Work

Maria
Lupe
Daniel
Kim

They can hop fast.
They eat plants.
They eat pellets.
You can catch some.
Their ears are pink
   on the inside.
They dig holes.
They are soft and
   fluffy, because of
   their fur.
They have big ears.
They come in all
   colors.

born? alive

Why are there
different colors of
fur? because there are
different kinds of rabbits.

How do they protect
   themselves?
camouflage

How do their feet work?

What do you call a
male rabbit?

What do you call a
female rabbit?

What do you call a
baby rabbit?

Some teachers teach one subject.

Some teachers teach many subjects.

Teachers help students work together.

Teachers help students want to learn.

# Words to Know

**classroom**—a room in a school where classes take place; some teachers teach in one classroom and others teach in many classrooms.

**lesson**—a set of skills or facts taught at one time; teachers prepare lessons for each day of class.

**plan**—to decide how something will be done; teachers plan lessons and activities for students.

**student**—a person who goes to a school to learn; teachers help students learn.

**subject**—an area of study such as reading, mathematics, or history

**supplies**—items needed to perform a task; teachers have books, paper, computers, and other supplies in classrooms.

**teacher**—a person who helps others learn and solve problems; teachers encourage students to want to learn.

# Read More

**Deedrick, Tami.** *Teachers.* Community Helpers. Mankato, Minn.: Bridgestone Books, 1998.

**Greene, Carol.** *Teachers Help Us Learn.* Community Helpers. Chanhassen, Minn.: Child's World, 1998.

**Weber, Valerie and Gloria Jenkins.** *School in Grandma's Day.* In Grandma's Day. Minneapolis: Carolrhoda Books, 1999.

# Internet Sites

FactHound offers a safe, fun way to find Internet sites related to this book. All of the sites on FactHound have been researched by our staff.

Here's how:

1. Visit *www.facthound.com*

2. Type in this special code **0736805338** for age-appropriate sites. Or enter a search word related to this book for a more general search.

3. Click on the **Fetch It** button.

FactHound will fetch the best sites for you!

# Index/Word List

**Word Count: 38**
**Early-Intervention Level: 7**

**Editorial Credits**
Martha E. H. Rustad, editor; Abby Bradford, Bradfordesign, Inc., cover designer; Kia
Bielke, production designer; Kimberly Danger, photo researcher

**Photo Credits**
International Stock/George Ancona, 14, 16
Jim Cummins/FPG International LLC, cover
Kim Stanton, 6, 8
Mark Adams/FPG International LLC, 20
Shaffer Photography/James L. Shaffer, 18
Unicorn Stock Photos/Jeff Greenberg, 10; Martin Jones, 12
Uniphoto/Bob Daemmrich, 4
Visuals Unlimited/Nancy Alexander, 1